Bouncing Back: Overcom
Building Resilience in

Gabriela Petrova

Copyright © [2023]

Title: Bouncing Back: Overcoming Obstacles and Building Resilience in Everyday Life

Author's: Gabriela Petrova.

This book was printed and published by [Publisher's: Gabriela Petrova] in [2023]

ISBN:

TABLE OF CONTENTS

Chapter 2: Identifying Obstacles

Recognizing Common Obstacles

Common challenges faced in everyday life

Identifying personal obstacles and their impact

Understanding the Power of Perspective

Shifting perspective to view obstacles as opportunities for growth

Overcoming negative thinking patterns

Chapter 3: Building Resilience

Developing Emotional Intelligence

Understanding and managing emotions effectively

Building self-awareness and empathy

Cultivating a Growth Mindset

Embracing challenges and learning from failures

Nurturing a belief in personal growth and development

Chapter 4: Strategies for Overcoming Obstacles 49

Building a Supportive Network

The importance of a strong support system

Cultivating healthy relationships and seeking help when needed

Practicing Self-Care

Prioritizing physical and mental well-being

Strategies for self-care and stress management

Chapter 5: Resilience in Action 65

Learning from Resilient Individuals

Inspiring stories of individuals who have overcome significant obstacles

Lessons learned and key takeaways

Applying Resilience in Everyday Life

Practical tips for applying resilience in various areas of life (work, relationships, personal growth)

Setting goals and taking action towards resilience

Conclusion

Recap of key concepts and strategies discussed

Encouragement to continue building resilience in everyday life

Title: Bouncing Back: Overcoming Obstacles and Building Resilience in Everyday Life

Introduction:

In our journey through life, we often encounter obstacles that test our resilience and determination. This subchapter, titled "Bouncing Back: Overcoming Obstacles and Building Resilience in Everyday Life," is a guide to help you navigate these challenges and unlock your true potential. No matter who you are or what your aspirations may be, this chapter is designed to inspire and empower you to achieve your best.

Overcoming   Obstacles:

Life is filled with setbacks, disappointments, and unexpected challenges. However, it is not the obstacles themselves that define us but rather how we respond to them. This subchapter provides valuable insights into the mindset required to overcome obstacles and bounce back stronger than ever. By adopting a positive outlook and nurturing resilience, you can turn setbacks into stepping stones towards success.

Building   Resilience:

Resilience is the ability to bounce back from adversity and maintain a positive attitude amidst difficult circumstances. In this subchapter, we explore various strategies and techniques to build resilience in everyday life. From cultivating a growth mindset to practicing self-care and seeking support from loved ones, you will learn how to develop the emotional strength necessary to weather any storm.

Unleashing   Your   Potential:

Each of us possesses untapped potential waiting to be unleashed. However, fear, self-doubt, and limiting beliefs often hold us back from achieving our best. This subchapter provides practical tips and exercises to help you break free from these barriers and tap into your full potential. By recognizing your strengths, setting clear goals, and embracing failure as a stepping stone to growth, you can unleash the greatness within you.

Achieving   Your   Best:
Ultimately, the purpose of this subchapter is to guide you towards achieving your best in all areas of life. Whether you are striving for career success, personal growth, or improved relationships, the principles shared within these pages are universally applicable. By developing resilience, overcoming obstacles, and unleashing your potential, you will find yourself better equipped to navigate life's challenges and seize opportunities with confidence and determination.

Conclusion:
Life is unpredictable, and it is through adversity that we grow and become stronger. "Bouncing Back: Overcoming Obstacles and Building Resilience in Everyday Life" is a book that speaks to everyone, offering valuable insights and practical advice on how to overcome obstacles, build resilience, and achieve your best. By embracing the principles outlined in this subchapter, you will be empowered to face life's challenges head-on, bounce back from setbacks, and create a life filled with success and fulfillment. So, take the first step towards unlocking your true potential and start bouncing back today!

Introduction

Welcome and brief explanation of the purpose of the book

Welcome to "Bouncing Back: Overcoming Obstacles and Building Resilience in Everyday Life." This book is designed to help you achieve your best by providing you with the tools and strategies to overcome any obstacles that come your way. Whether you are a student, a professional, a stay-at-home parent, or anyone looking to improve their resilience, this book is for you.

In this subchapter, we would like to extend a warm welcome and provide a brief explanation of the purpose of this book. We believe that life is full of challenges, and it is how we bounce back from these challenges that determines our success and happiness. Resilience is not something we are born with; it is a skill that can be learned and developed throughout our lives.

The purpose of this book is to empower and inspire you to overcome adversity and build resilience in your everyday life. We understand that everyone faces different obstacles, whether it is a setback at work, a personal loss, or a health issue. However, by developing resilience, you can navigate these challenges with strength, determination, and optimism.

In the following chapters, we will explore various techniques and strategies that will help you bounce back from setbacks, cultivate a positive mindset, and develop the resilience needed to achieve your best. We will delve into the power of self-reflection and self-awareness, explore the importance of setting realistic goals, and provide practical exercises to enhance your problem-solving skills.

Moreover, we will share inspiring stories of individuals who have faced tremendous adversity and managed to bounce back stronger than ever. These stories will serve as a reminder that resilience is within reach for everyone, regardless of their circumstances.

We invite you to embark on this journey towards building resilience and achieving your best. By the end of this book, you will have gained valuable insights and practical tools to navigate life's challenges with resilience and grace. Remember, setbacks are not permanent roadblocks but opportunities for growth. Let's bounce back together and create a life filled with resilience, fulfillment, and success.

Importance of developing resilience in navigating life's challenges

Resilience is the key to not only surviving but thriving in the face of life's challenges. In the book "Bouncing Back: Overcoming Obstacles and Building Resilience in Everyday Life," we explore the significance of developing resilience and how it can help you achieve your best in all aspects of life. This subchapter delves into the importance of resilience and its impact on navigating life's challenges.

Life is full of ups and downs, and no one is exempt from facing difficulties. However, it is how we respond to these challenges that determines our overall success and happiness. Developing resilience equips you with the tools to bounce back from setbacks, adapt to change, and persevere through adversity.

Resilience allows you to maintain a positive mindset even in the face of adversity. It helps you cultivate the belief that you have the strength and ability to overcome any obstacle that comes your way. This mindset not only enhances your mental well-being but also fuels your motivation and determination to achieve your best.

Furthermore, resilience helps you develop effective problem-solving skills. Instead of viewing challenges as insurmountable roadblocks, a resilient individual sees them as opportunities for growth and learning. This enables you to approach problems with a solution-oriented mindset, finding creative and innovative ways to overcome them. By developing resilience, you become more adept at finding alternative paths and adapting to changing circumstances, enhancing your chances of achieving your goals.

Resilience also plays a vital role in building and maintaining healthy relationships. Life's challenges can often strain our connections with others, but resilience allows us to navigate these difficulties with grace and understanding. It helps us communicate effectively, manage conflicts, and seek support when needed. By developing resilience in our relationships, we foster deeper connections and create a solid support system that can help us through tough times.

In conclusion, developing resilience is crucial for achieving your best in life. It enables you to maintain a positive mindset, develop problem-solving skills, and build and maintain healthy relationships. By embracing resilience, you become better equipped to navigate life's challenges, bouncing back stronger and more determined than ever before. So, start developing your resilience today and unlock your full potential to overcome any obstacle and achieve your best in all areas of life.

Chapter 1: Understanding Resilience

What is Resilience?

Resilience is a fundamental trait that allows individuals to bounce back from adversity and overcome obstacles in everyday life. It is the ability to adapt and thrive in the face of adversity, setbacks, and challenges. Resilience is not about avoiding difficulties or pretending that they don't exist; instead, it is about developing a mindset and set of skills that enable you to navigate through life's ups and downs with grace and determination.

In the book "Bouncing Back: Overcoming Obstacles and Building Resilience in Everyday Life," we delve into the concept of resilience to help you understand its importance and how to cultivate it in your own life. Whether you are seeking personal growth, professional success, or simply want to achieve your best, resilience is a key ingredient to unlocking your full potential.

Resilience encompasses several core elements that are essential for achieving your best. First and foremost, it is about developing a positive and growth-oriented mindset. By reframing setbacks as opportunities for learning and growth, you can turn challenges into stepping stones towards success. Resilient individuals have the ability to adapt to new situations, embrace change, and see failure as a temporary setback rather than a permanent defeat.

Another critical aspect of resilience is developing a strong support system. Surrounding yourself with positive and supportive people who believe in your abilities can make a world of difference when facing adversity. These trusted individuals can provide guidance, encouragement, and a listening ear when you need it most. Additionally, building resilience involves cultivating strong emotional intelligence and self-awareness, which enables you to understand and manage your emotions effectively.

Resilience is not a fixed trait that some are born with and others lack; it is a skill that can be learned and developed over time. Through practical strategies, exercises, and real-life examples, "Bouncing Back" provides you with the tools to enhance your resilience and achieve your best in all areas of life.

Whether you are facing a personal setback, a professional challenge, or simply want to build a more resilient mindset, this subchapter will serve as a guide to understanding what resilience is and how it can transform your life. By embracing resilience, you can navigate life's obstacles with confidence, bounce back from setbacks stronger than ever, and ultimately achieve your best self.

Definition and characteristics of resilience

Resilience is a term that is often thrown around when discussing personal development and achieving success. But what exactly does it mean to be resilient? In this subchapter, we will delve into the definition and characteristics of resilience, helping you understand how it can be a powerful tool in achieving your best in everyday life.

Resilience, at its core, refers to the ability to bounce back from adversity and recover quickly from setbacks. It is the mental and emotional strength that enables individuals to face challenges head-on, adapt to change, and persevere in the face of adversity. Resilient individuals possess a unique set of characteristics that enable them to navigate life's ups and downs with grace and determination.

One key characteristic of resilience is optimism. Resilient people have a positive outlook on life, even during difficult times. They believe in their ability to overcome obstacles and view setbacks as temporary rather than permanent. This optimistic mindset allows them to stay motivated and focused on their goals, regardless of the challenges they may encounter.

Another important characteristic of resilience is adaptability. Resilient individuals are able to quickly adjust their plans and strategies when faced with unexpected circumstances. They understand that change is inevitable and instead of resisting it, they embrace it as an opportunity for growth. By being flexible and open-minded, they can find new and innovative ways to overcome obstacles and achieve their best.

Resilient people also possess a strong sense of self-belief. They have confidence in their abilities and trust themselves to make the right decisions. This self-assurance allows them to stay motivated and persevere, even when faced with self-doubt or criticism from others. They understand that setbacks are a part of the journey, and their unwavering self-belief helps them stay resilient in the face of adversity.

Lastly, resilience is closely tied to emotional intelligence. Resilient individuals are aware of their emotions and can effectively manage them, even in challenging situations. They have a high level of self-awareness and are able to regulate their emotions to avoid becoming overwhelmed or reactive. This emotional intelligence enables them to approach setbacks with a calm and rational mindset, making it easier for them to bounce back and maintain their focus on achieving their best.

In conclusion, resilience is a powerful trait that can help individuals overcome obstacles and achieve their best in everyday life. By embracing optimism, adaptability, self-belief, and emotional intelligence, anyone can cultivate resilience and develop the strength to bounce back from adversity. So, remember, no matter what challenges you may face, building resilience will empower you to overcome them and thrive in every aspect of your life.

The role of resilience in overcoming obstacles

Resilience is a fundamental quality that plays a crucial role in helping individuals overcome obstacles and achieve their best in life. In the face of adversity, resilience enables individuals to bounce back, to rise above challenges, and to keep moving forward in pursuit of their goals and dreams. Whether it is a setback at work, a personal loss, or a major life change, resilience empowers individuals to navigate through difficult times and emerge stronger on the other side.

One of the key aspects of resilience is the ability to adapt to change. Life is full of unexpected twists and turns, and those who are resilient have the capacity to embrace change and find ways to thrive in new circumstances. Instead of getting stuck in a cycle of despair and self-pity, resilient individuals approach challenges with a growth mindset, viewing them as opportunities for personal growth and development. By reframing setbacks as learning experiences, they are able to extract valuable lessons and apply them to future situations, ultimately achieving their best.

Resilience also involves the ability to maintain a positive outlook, even in the face of adversity. By cultivating a resilient mindset, individuals can effectively manage stress, remain optimistic, and find creative solutions to problems. Instead of dwelling on failures or dwelling on negative emotions, resilient individuals focus on their strengths and build upon them. They understand that setbacks are temporary and view them as stepping stones on the path to success.

Furthermore, resilience is closely tied to perseverance. It is the ability to keep going, to never give up, even when faced with seemingly insurmountable obstacles. Resilient individuals are not deterred by setbacks or failures; instead, they use these experiences as fuel to propel themselves forward. Their determination and unwavering commitment to their goals enable them to push through challenges and achieve their best.

In conclusion, resilience is an essential quality for achieving one's best in life. It enables individuals to adapt to change, maintain a positive outlook, and persevere through difficulties. By cultivating resilience, individuals can overcome obstacles, bounce back from setbacks, and ultimately reach their full potential. No matter what challenges life throws their way, those who possess resilience have the strength and mindset to rise above and achieve greatness.

The Benefits of Building Resilience

In today's fast-paced and unpredictable world, the ability to bounce back from setbacks and overcome obstacles is becoming increasingly crucial. Building resilience is not only essential for achieving your best but also for maintaining your mental and emotional well-being. In this subchapter, we will explore the numerous benefits of developing resilience and how it can positively impact various aspects of your life.

One of the primary advantages of building resilience is the ability to adapt to change. Life is full of unexpected twists and turns, and those who are resilient can quickly adjust their mindset and approach when faced with new challenges. Instead of being paralyzed by fear or disappointment, resilient individuals view obstacles as opportunities for growth and learning. They are better equipped to handle change and can embrace it, ultimately leading to personal and professional growth.

Furthermore, resilience can enhance your problem-solving skills. When confronted with a difficult situation, resilient individuals are more likely to remain calm and think critically. They possess the mental flexibility to explore alternative solutions and find new perspectives. This ability to approach problems with a clear and level-headed mindset allows them to make effective decisions, leading to better outcomes.

Another benefit of resilience is the positive impact it has on relationships. Resilient individuals tend to have stronger social connections and support networks. Their ability to navigate challenges and maintain a positive outlook attracts others who seek guidance and inspiration. By building resilience, you can cultivate meaningful relationships and surround yourself with individuals who uplift and empower you.

Moreover, resilience has a profound impact on mental health. It acts as a protective factor against stress, anxiety, and depression. Resilient individuals are better equipped to manage and cope with emotional distress, maintaining a sense of balance and well-being even during challenging times. By developing resilience, you can improve your overall mental health and build emotional strength.

In conclusion, building resilience offers a multitude of benefits that can positively impact various areas of your life. By embracing change, enhancing problem-solving skills, fostering strong relationships, and improving mental health, you can achieve your best and thrive in everyday life. Resilience is not only a valuable tool for overcoming obstacles but also a key component of personal growth and happiness. So, let us embark on this journey together and discover the power of resilience in bouncing back from life's challenges.

How resilience positively impacts mental and emotional well-being

In today's fast-paced and unpredictable world, it is not uncommon to face various challenges and obstacles that can take a toll on our mental and emotional well-being. Whether it is a setback at work, a personal loss, or a global crisis, life can throw curveballs at us when we least expect it. However, the ability to bounce back from these adversities is what sets apart individuals who thrive from those who merely survive. This subchapter titled "How resilience positively impacts mental and emotional well-being" aims to shed light on the crucial role resilience plays in achieving our best and attaining overall well-being.

Resilience can be defined as the capacity to adapt and recover from difficult situations, adversity, or trauma. It is not about avoiding stress or hardships, but rather about building a strong foundation that allows us to withstand and overcome these challenges. Resilience serves as a protective shield for our mental and emotional health, enabling us to maintain a positive outlook and navigate through life's ups and downs with greater ease.

One of the key ways resilience positively impacts mental and emotional well-being is by enhancing our ability to manage stress. Resilient individuals have developed effective coping mechanisms that enable them to regulate their emotions and reduce the negative impact of stressors. They possess a sense of control over their lives, which helps them approach difficult circumstances with a problem-solving mindset rather than feeling overwhelmed or helpless.

Moreover, resilience fosters a growth mindset, which is essential for achieving our best. Resilient individuals view setbacks and failures as opportunities for learning and personal growth, rather than as permanent roadblocks. They possess a strong belief in their abilities to overcome obstacles, which fuels their motivation and determination to strive for success. This mindset enables them to embrace challenges, take calculated risks, and constantly push their limits, leading to continuous self-improvement.

Resilience also plays a vital role in fostering positive relationships and social support networks. When faced with adversity, resilient individuals tend to seek support from others rather than isolating themselves. They understand the importance of connection and are willing to reach out for help when needed. By building and maintaining strong relationships, they create a support system that can provide emotional comfort and practical assistance during challenging times.

In conclusion, resilience is a powerful tool that positively impacts our mental and emotional well-being. By developing resilience, we can effectively manage stress, foster a growth mindset, and build strong relationships. It enables us to bounce back from setbacks, overcome obstacles, and achieve our best in every aspect of life. Cultivating resilience is a lifelong journey, and by embracing it, we can navigate through the ups and downs of life with resilience, strength, and grace.

Improved problem-solving abilities and adaptability

Improved problem-solving abilities and adaptability are crucial skills for achieving your best in every aspect of life. In the face of challenges and obstacles, these capabilities allow you to bounce back and find creative solutions, ultimately leading to personal growth and success.

Problem-solving is an essential skill that enables individuals to identify, analyze, and resolve complex issues. It involves applying logical thinking, critical analysis, and creativity to overcome obstacles. By cultivating problem-solving abilities, you can tackle any situation with confidence and effectiveness. Whether it's a work-related problem, a personal dilemma, or even a global crisis, your problem-solving skills will help you navigate through uncertainty.

One key aspect of problem-solving is adaptability. In today's fast-paced world, being adaptable is essential for thriving in any environment. Adaptability allows you to quickly adjust to new circumstances, embrace change, and find innovative solutions. It enables you to view challenges as opportunities for growth, rather than setbacks. When you approach problems with adaptability, you are more likely to find unique perspectives and uncover hidden possibilities.

By developing problem-solving abilities and adaptability, you can enhance your overall performance, achieve your goals, and even exceed your own expectations. These skills empower you to think critically, make informed decisions, and take calculated risks. They enable you to overcome obstacles that may have otherwise seemed insurmountable, propelling you towards personal and professional growth.

Furthermore, problem-solving abilities and adaptability are not only beneficial for individual success but also for collective progress. In an interconnected world, collaboration and teamwork are essential. By honing these skills, you become a valuable asset in any team or organization. Your ability to navigate complex problems and adapt to changing circumstances brings innovative solutions and fosters a positive work culture.

In conclusion, improved problem-solving abilities and adaptability are indispensable skills for achieving your best in every aspect of life. These skills empower you to overcome obstacles, embrace change, and find innovative solutions. By cultivating these capabilities, you can drive personal growth, exceed your own expectations, and contribute to the collective progress. So, embrace challenges with a problem-solving mindset, be adaptable in the face of change, and unlock your true potential.

Chapter 2: Identifying Obstacles

Recognizing Common Obstacles

In our journey towards achieving our best selves, we often come across various obstacles that can hinder our progress and test our resilience. It is crucial to recognize these common obstacles so that we can develop effective strategies to overcome them and continue moving forward on our path to success.

One of the most common obstacles we encounter is fear. Fear can be paralyzing, preventing us from taking risks and stepping outside our comfort zones. Whether it's fear of failure, fear of judgment, or fear of the unknown, it is important to acknowledge and confront these fears head-on. By understanding that fear is a natural part of growth, we can learn to embrace it and use it as a driving force to propel us forward.

Another obstacle that often stands in our way is self-doubt. We tend to underestimate our abilities and question our worthiness of achieving our goals. Overcoming self-doubt requires a shift in mindset and a belief in our own capabilities. By practicing self-compassion, setting realistic expectations, and surrounding ourselves with positive influences, we can gradually build our self-confidence and overcome this common obstacle.

Procrastination is yet another obstacle that can hinder our progress. We often find ourselves putting off important tasks and prioritizing less important ones. Recognizing this tendency is the first step towards overcoming it. By breaking tasks into smaller, manageable steps, setting deadlines, and holding ourselves accountable, we can combat procrastination and make consistent progress towards our goals.

In addition to fear, self-doubt, and procrastination, other common obstacles we may encounter include lack of motivation, negative self-talk, and external distractions. It is essential to be aware of these obstacles and develop strategies to overcome them. This may involve seeking support from mentors, creating a positive and inspiring environment, and practicing mindfulness and self-reflection to stay focused and motivated.

Recognizing and acknowledging these common obstacles is the first step towards building resilience and overcoming them. By understanding that obstacles are a natural part of the journey towards achieving our best, we can view them as opportunities for growth and development. With determination, perseverance, and a positive mindset, we can bounce back from any setback and continue on our path towards success.

Common challenges faced in everyday life

Life is full of ups and downs, and everyone faces their fair share of challenges on a daily basis. These challenges can vary greatly from person to person, but there are some common hurdles that many of us encounter. In this subchapter, we will explore these challenges and provide insights on how to overcome them, with the goal of helping you achieve your best in everyday life.

One of the most common challenges people face is stress. Whether it's due to work pressure, financial worries, or personal relationships, stress can take a toll on our physical and mental well-being. However, by adopting healthy coping mechanisms such as exercise, meditation, and time management techniques, we can effectively manage stress and prevent it from overwhelming us.

Another challenge that often arises is the lack of motivation and self-discipline. It can be difficult to stay focused and driven towards our goals when faced with distractions and setbacks. However, by setting realistic and achievable goals, breaking them down into smaller tasks, and celebrating each milestone, we can maintain our motivation and develop the self-discipline needed to achieve our best.

In addition, interpersonal relationships can pose challenges in our everyday lives. Communication issues, conflicts, and misunderstandings are all too common in our interactions with others. Learning effective communication skills, practicing empathy, and embracing conflict resolution techniques can greatly improve our relationships and overall well-being.

Time management is another challenge that many people struggle with. The demands of work, family, and personal commitments can often leave us feeling overwhelmed and unable to prioritize effectively. By learning to prioritize tasks, delegate when necessary, and set boundaries, we can regain control of our time and achieve a better work-life balance.

Lastly, fear of failure can hinder our progress and prevent us from reaching our full potential. It is important to remember that failure is a natural part of life and essential for growth. By reframing our mindset, embracing a growth mindset, and learning from our mistakes, we can bounce back from failure and use it as a stepping stone to success.

In conclusion, everyday life is filled with challenges that can hinder our progress and well-being. However, by acknowledging these common challenges and implementing strategies to overcome them, we can build resilience and achieve our best. Remember, it's not about avoiding challenges but rather about bouncing back stronger each time.

Identifying personal obstacles and their impact

In our journey towards achieving our best, we often encounter obstacles that hinder our progress. These obstacles can manifest in various forms, including external challenges and internal struggles. To overcome these hurdles and build resilience in everyday life, it is crucial to first identify these personal obstacles and understand their impact on our growth.

External obstacles can arise from our environment, such as financial constraints, lack of opportunities, or unsupportive relationships. These challenges can be daunting, but recognizing them as external factors allows us to separate them from our own abilities and potential. By acknowledging these obstacles, we can develop strategies to navigate around them or find ways to overcome them altogether.

On the other hand, internal obstacles stem from within ourselves – our fears, self-doubts, limiting beliefs, and negative thought patterns. These personal barriers often have a more profound impact on our growth as they directly affect our mindset and self-perception. Identifying these internal obstacles is essential for building resilience because it helps us confront and challenge our own limitations.

Understanding the impact of these obstacles is crucial in our journey towards self-improvement. External obstacles can hinder our progress, but they also present opportunities for growth and learning. By recognizing the impact they have on our lives, we can develop strategies to adapt and find alternative paths to success.

Internal obstacles, on the other hand, can be deeply ingrained and may require significant introspection and self-reflection to overcome. They can undermine our self-confidence, hinder decision-making, and limit our ability to take risks. By identifying these barriers, we can work on developing self-compassion, challenging our negative beliefs, and cultivating a growth mindset.

Recognizing and understanding personal obstacles is the first step towards building resilience and achieving our best. It allows us to take ownership of our challenges and empowers us to find creative solutions. By acknowledging the impact these obstacles have on our lives, we can develop strategies to overcome them, seek support from others, and cultivate the resilience needed to bounce back from setbacks.

In the following chapters, we will delve deeper into specific techniques and approaches to overcome these personal obstacles and build resilience. By embracing a growth mindset and developing self-awareness, we can navigate the hurdles that come our way, achieve our goals, and thrive in every aspect of our lives. Remember, it is not the absence of obstacles that defines our success, but our ability to overcome them and bounce back stronger than ever.

Understanding the Power of Perspective

In our journey towards achieving our best, one of the most valuable tools we can possess is the power of perspective. How we view and interpret the world around us greatly influences our ability to overcome obstacles and build resilience in everyday life. Our perspective shapes our thoughts, emotions, and actions, ultimately determining our level of success and fulfillment.

Perspective is the lens through which we see the world. It is our unique way of understanding and making sense of our experiences. However, it is important to recognize that our perspective is not fixed, but rather, it can be shaped and molded. By consciously choosing to adopt a positive and growth-oriented perspective, we can transform how we navigate challenges and setbacks.

One key aspect of understanding the power of perspective is recognizing that there are often multiple ways to interpret a situation. What may appear as a failure or setback at first glance can be reframed as an opportunity for growth and learning. By consciously choosing to view obstacles as stepping stones rather than roadblocks, we can cultivate a mindset of resilience and perseverance.

Shifting our perspective also allows us to see the bigger picture. When faced with difficulties, it can be easy to get caught up in the moment and lose sight of our long-term goals. By stepping back and gaining a broader perspective, we can gain clarity and make more informed decisions. This helps us stay focused on our aspirations and take necessary steps towards achieving our best.

Moreover, perspective plays a crucial role in how we perceive ourselves and our abilities. A positive perspective empowers us to believe in our capabilities and have faith in our potential for growth. It enables us to approach challenges with confidence and a willingness to learn from our mistakes. On the other hand, a negative perspective can lead to self-doubt and a fear of failure, hindering our progress.

In conclusion, understanding the power of perspective is essential for achieving our best. By consciously choosing a positive and growth-oriented perspective, we can transform obstacles into opportunities, gain a broader view of our goals, and develop a strong belief in our abilities. So, let us embrace the power of perspective and bounce back from any challenges that come our way, building resilience in our everyday lives.

Shifting perspective to view obstacles as opportunities for growth

In the journey of achieving your best, obstacles are bound to arise. They can sometimes be overwhelming, causing us to doubt ourselves and our abilities. However, what if we could shift our perspective and view these obstacles as opportunities for growth? What if we could turn adversity into a stepping stone towards our goals? This subchapter aims to explore this powerful mindset shift and provide practical strategies to help you embrace obstacles and build resilience in everyday life.

Obstacles are often seen as roadblocks, hindrances that prevent us from reaching our desired destination. But what if we start seeing them as opportunities? Opportunities to learn, to adapt, and to become stronger versions of ourselves. When we shift our perspective and view obstacles as stepping stones, we open ourselves up to a world of possibilities.

One way to embrace obstacles is by reframing our mindset. Instead of feeling defeated, we can choose to see obstacles as challenges that will push us to grow and expand our capabilities. By adopting a growth mindset, we can approach obstacles with curiosity and a willingness to learn, rather than succumbing to frustration and despair.

Another powerful strategy is to reframe failure as feedback. When we encounter setbacks or face failures, it's easy to let them define us and our abilities. However, by reframing failure as feedback, we can extract valuable lessons from our experiences and use them to improve and grow. Every obstacle becomes an opportunity to reflect, reassess, and refine our approach.

Moreover, it is essential to cultivate resilience in the face of obstacles. Resilience is the ability to bounce back from setbacks and challenges. It allows us to persevere, adapt, and find new ways forward. By building resilience, we develop the strength and determination to overcome any obstacle that comes our way.

Practical exercises and techniques are also included in this subchapter to help you shift your perspective and embrace obstacles. These exercises will guide you in developing a growth mindset, reframing failures, and building resilience. By integrating these strategies into your daily life, you will be better equipped to navigate obstacles and achieve your best.

In conclusion, obstacles are not roadblocks but opportunities for growth. By shifting our perspective and viewing obstacles as stepping stones, we can harness their power to propel us forward. This subchapter aims to empower you with the mindset and strategies necessary to embrace obstacles, learn from them, and build resilience in everyday life. Remember, it is through facing and overcoming obstacles that we truly achieve our best.

Overcoming negative thinking patterns

In our journey to achieving our best, negative thinking patterns can often become a major obstacle. These patterns can manifest in various ways, such as self-doubt, fear of failure, or a constant focus on the negatives in life. However, with the right mindset and strategies, we can learn to overcome these negative thinking patterns and build resilience in our everyday lives.

One powerful technique to counter negative thinking patterns is to practice self-awareness. By becoming more aware of our thoughts and the impact they have on our emotions and actions, we can start to challenge and reframe negative thoughts. This involves consciously questioning the validity of our negative beliefs and replacing them with more positive and empowering ones. For example, instead of thinking, "I will never succeed," we can reframe it as, "I am capable of overcoming challenges and achieving my goals."

Another effective method is to surround ourselves with positivity. This can be achieved by seeking out inspirational and motivational resources, such as books, podcasts, or even supportive friends and mentors. By immersing ourselves in a positive environment, we can counteract the influence of negative thinking patterns and cultivate a more optimistic mindset.

Additionally, practicing gratitude has been proven to be a powerful antidote to negative thinking. By regularly acknowledging and appreciating the positive aspects of our lives, we can shift our focus away from negativity and promote a more positive outlook. Keeping a gratitude journal or simply taking a few moments each day to reflect on what we are grateful for can make a significant difference in our mindset.

Furthermore, it is essential to challenge our limiting beliefs. Often, negative thinking patterns are rooted in deeply ingrained beliefs about ourselves and our capabilities. By examining these beliefs and questioning their accuracy, we can open ourselves up to new possibilities and overcome self-imposed limitations.

Remember, overcoming negative thinking patterns is a journey that requires patience, consistency, and self-compassion. It takes time to rewire our brains and establish new thought patterns. However, with dedication and perseverance, we can gradually transform our mindset and build resilience to achieve our best in all areas of life.

In summary, overcoming negative thinking patterns is crucial for achieving our best. By practicing self-awareness, surrounding ourselves with positivity, cultivating gratitude, and challenging our limiting beliefs, we can break free from the shackles of negativity and build resilience in our everyday lives. So, let us embark on this transformative journey and embrace the power of a positive mindset to bounce back from any obstacle that comes our way.

Chapter 3: Building Resilience

Developing Emotional Intelligence

Emotional intelligence is a crucial skill that plays a significant role in achieving success and personal growth. In the subchapter "Developing Emotional Intelligence" of the book "Bouncing Back: Overcoming Obstacles and Building Resilience in Everyday Life," we delve into the importance of emotional intelligence and provide valuable insights and strategies for enhancing this essential trait.

Emotional intelligence is the ability to recognize and manage our emotions effectively, as well as understand and empathize with the emotions of others. It involves being aware of our own feelings, controlling our impulses, and building strong relationships based on empathy and effective communication. Developing emotional intelligence can significantly impact various aspects of our lives, including personal relationships, work performance, and overall well-being.

In this subchapter, we will explore the different components of emotional intelligence and how each one contributes to achieving our best. We will discuss self-awareness, self-regulation, motivation, empathy, and social skills, providing practical tips and exercises to enhance these areas.

Self-awareness is the foundation of emotional intelligence, as it involves understanding our own emotions, strengths, weaknesses, and values. By developing self-awareness, we can better understand our reactions and make conscious choices that align with our goals and values.

Self-regulation is the ability to manage and control our emotions, thoughts, and behaviors effectively. It allows us to handle stressful situations with composure, make rational decisions, and adapt to changes. We will explore techniques such as deep breathing, mindfulness, and reframing negative thoughts to strengthen our self-regulation skills.

Motivation is another crucial component of emotional intelligence. By cultivating a growth mindset, setting meaningful goals, and finding intrinsic motivation, we can overcome obstacles and persevere in achieving our best.

Empathy is the ability to understand and share the feelings of others. We will discuss the importance of active listening, non-verbal cues, and perspective-taking to develop empathy and build strong, supportive relationships.

Lastly, we will delve into social skills and effective communication. Developing these skills allows us to navigate conflicts, collaborate with others, and build a network of supportive individuals who can contribute to our personal and professional growth.

By developing emotional intelligence, we can unlock our full potential and achieve our best in all areas of life. This subchapter aims to provide practical tools and insights to help every reader enhance their emotional intelligence and thrive in their personal and professional endeavors.

Understanding and managing emotions effectively

Emotions are an integral part of our lives. They influence our thoughts, behavior, and overall well-being. Whether it's happiness, sadness, anger, or fear, each emotion serves a purpose and provides valuable information about our current state. Learning to understand and manage our emotions effectively is vital for achieving our best and building resilience in everyday life.

The first step towards understanding emotions is to recognize and acknowledge them. Often, we tend to suppress or ignore certain emotions, which can lead to a buildup of negative energy. By paying attention to our emotional experiences, we can gain insight into what triggers them and how they impact our thoughts and actions.

Once we have identified our emotions, the next step is to explore their underlying causes. Emotions are not random; they are responses to certain events or situations. Understanding the root causes of our emotions helps us address them more effectively. It could be a past trauma, an unresolved conflict, or even an unmet need. By delving deeper into our emotions, we can gain a better understanding of ourselves and our triggers.

Managing emotions effectively requires adopting healthy coping strategies. Instead of allowing emotions to control us, we need to take charge and respond in a constructive manner. This involves developing emotional intelligence, which includes skills like self-awareness, self-regulation, empathy, and effective communication. By enhancing our emotional intelligence, we can navigate through difficult situations with greater ease.

Practicing self-care is another crucial aspect of managing emotions effectively. Engaging in activities that bring us joy, relaxation, and a sense of fulfillment helps us maintain emotional balance. This could include hobbies, exercise, spending time with loved ones, or seeking professional help when needed. Taking care of our physical, mental, and emotional well-being lays a strong foundation for emotional resilience.

Building resilience in the face of adversity also requires reframing our mindset towards emotions. Emotions are not weaknesses; they are indicators of our humanity. Embracing our emotions and accepting them as a part of our experience allows us to develop a healthier relationship with them. By viewing emotions as opportunities for growth and learning, we can bounce back from setbacks and turn challenges into opportunities.

In conclusion, understanding and managing emotions effectively is essential for achieving our best and building resilience in everyday life. By recognizing, exploring, and managing our emotions, we can gain valuable insights, respond constructively, and maintain emotional balance. Emotions are not to be feared or suppressed but embraced and understood. With the right mindset and coping strategies, we can overcome obstacles and thrive in every aspect of our lives.

Building self-awareness and empathy

In our journey to achieve our best, it is essential to build self-awareness and empathy. These two qualities are the foundation for personal growth, resilience, and successful relationships. In this subchapter, we will explore how developing self-awareness and empathy can help us overcome obstacles and bounce back from adversity in everyday life.

Self-awareness is the ability to recognize and understand our own emotions, thoughts, and behaviors. It involves being in tune with our strengths, weaknesses, values, and beliefs. By developing self-awareness, we gain a clearer understanding of who we are, what drives us, and how we can navigate through challenges.

One way to enhance self-awareness is through self-reflection. Taking time to pause and reflect on our experiences allows us to gain insights into our emotions, patterns, and reactions. Journaling, meditation, or seeking feedback from trusted individuals can also aid in this process. By becoming more self-aware, we can identify our triggers and make conscious choices that align with our values and goals.

Empathy, on the other hand, is the ability to understand and share the feelings of others. It involves putting ourselves in someone else's shoes, seeing the world from their perspective, and responding with compassion. Empathy enables us to build stronger connections with others, resolve conflicts, and provide support when needed.

To cultivate empathy, we must practice active listening and engage in open-minded conversations. By truly listening to others without judgment, we can gain a deeper understanding of their experiences and emotions. Empathy also involves being aware of non-verbal cues and paying attention to the subtle signals that indicate how someone is feeling.

By building self-awareness and empathy, we can navigate through life's challenges with greater resilience. Self-awareness allows us to recognize our emotions and triggers, enabling us to respond rather than react impulsively. Empathy, on the other hand, helps us build meaningful relationships, understand others' perspectives, and offer support during difficult times.

In conclusion, developing self-awareness and empathy is crucial for achieving our best in life. These qualities enable us to understand ourselves better, make conscious choices, and build strong connections with others. By incorporating self-reflection and active listening into our daily lives, we can enhance our resilience and bounce back from obstacles with grace and compassion. So let's embark on this journey of self-discovery and empathy, and watch as our lives transform for the better.

Cultivating a Growth Mindset

In the pursuit of achieving our best, one of the most crucial aspects is developing a growth mindset. This subchapter will delve into the concept of a growth mindset and provide valuable insights on how to cultivate it in our everyday lives. Whether you are a student, professional, entrepreneur, or anyone striving to reach their full potential, embracing a growth mindset can be transformative.

A growth mindset is the belief that our abilities and intelligence can be developed through dedication, hard work, and perseverance. It is the understanding that failure and setbacks are not permanent roadblocks but opportunities for learning and growth. With a growth mindset, we view challenges as stepping stones to success, and we embrace the process of continuous improvement.

To cultivate a growth mindset, it is essential to start by reframing our mindset from fixed to growth. Instead of believing that our abilities are fixed and limited, we must recognize that we have the power to develop and improve them. This shift in perspective opens up a world of possibilities and allows us to embrace challenges with enthusiasm and determination.

Another key aspect of cultivating a growth mindset is embracing failure as a stepping stone to success. Rather than viewing failure as a reflection of our abilities, we should see it as an opportunity to learn, adapt, and grow. By reframing failure as a necessary part of the learning process, we can overcome the fear of making mistakes and take calculated risks that lead to personal and professional growth.

Additionally, it is crucial to develop a passion for learning and self-improvement. A growth mindset thrives on the continuous pursuit of knowledge and skill development. Engage in activities that challenge you, seek out new experiences, and surround yourself with individuals who inspire and support your growth. By nurturing a love for learning, you will foster a growth mindset that propels you towards achieving your best.

Finally, cultivating a growth mindset requires a commitment to resilience and perseverance. Understand that success does not come overnight and setbacks are inevitable. However, with a growth mindset, you can bounce back from adversity, learn from failures, and continue moving forward towards your goals.

In conclusion, cultivating a growth mindset is a powerful tool for achieving your best. By reframing your mindset, embracing failure, nurturing a love for learning, and committing to resilience, you can unlock your full potential and overcome any obstacles that come your way. Embrace the process, stay determined, and watch as you continually grow and achieve greatness in every aspect of your life.

Embracing challenges and learning from failures

In our journey towards achieving our best, we often encounter numerous challenges and setbacks along the way. These obstacles can be disheartening and demotivating, but it is essential to remember that they are an integral part of life's learning process. In the subchapter "Embracing Challenges and Learning from Failures," we will explore the power of resilience and discuss strategies to bounce back stronger from setbacks.

Failure is not the end; it is merely a stepping stone towards success. It is through failures that we gain valuable insights, learn important lessons, and ultimately grow as individuals. Embracing challenges allows us to develop resilience, which is the key to overcoming obstacles and achieving our best.

One of the first steps in embracing challenges is to shift our mindset. Instead of viewing failures as personal shortcomings, we should see them as opportunities for growth. By reframing our perspective, we can learn to appreciate the lessons that failures offer, and use them as motivation to improve ourselves.

Another crucial aspect of embracing challenges is developing a growth mindset. This mindset believes that abilities and intelligence can be developed through dedication and hard work, rather than being fixed traits. By adopting a growth mindset, we can approach challenges with a sense of optimism and perseverance, knowing that our efforts will eventually yield positive results.

Learning from failures also involves reflecting on our experiences. Engaging in introspection allows us to identify the areas where we went wrong and understand what we can do differently next time. By analyzing our mistakes, we can make better-informed decisions and avoid repeating the same errors in the future.

Additionally, seeking support from others can greatly aid our journey towards embracing challenges. Surrounding ourselves with a strong support system of friends, mentors, or even online communities can provide us with guidance, motivation, and a fresh perspective when facing setbacks.

In conclusion, embracing challenges and learning from failures is an essential part of achieving our best. By shifting our mindset, developing a growth mindset, reflecting on our experiences, and seeking support, we can bounce back stronger from setbacks, overcome obstacles, and ultimately build resilience in our everyday lives. Remember, failure is not the end; it is an opportunity for growth and self-improvement. So, let us embrace challenges with open arms and learn from our failures, for they hold the keys to our future success.

Nurturing a belief in personal growth and development

Nurturing a belief in personal growth and development is essential for achieving your best in life. It is the driving force that propels us forward, helps us overcome obstacles, and builds our resilience. In the book "Bouncing Back: Overcoming Obstacles and Building Resilience in Everyday Life," we explore the power of nurturing this belief and how it can transform your life.

Believing in personal growth means recognizing that you have the potential to improve and develop in various areas of your life. It is about understanding that your abilities and skills are not fixed but can be enhanced through learning, practice, and perseverance. This mindset shift is crucial as it allows you to approach challenges with optimism and a willingness to learn, rather than being discouraged by setbacks.

One way to nurture this belief is by adopting a growth mindset. This concept, popularized by psychologist Carol Dweck, suggests that individuals who believe their abilities can be developed through hard work, dedication, and resilience are more likely to achieve their goals. By understanding that failure is not a permanent state but an opportunity for growth, you can cultivate a mindset that embraces challenges and sees setbacks as stepping stones towards success.

Another important aspect of nurturing a belief in personal growth and development is setting goals. By setting specific, achievable, and measurable goals, you create a roadmap for your personal growth journey. These goals should push you out of your comfort zone, allowing you to stretch and expand your capabilities. Celebrating small wins along the way will reinforce your belief in your ability to achieve your best.

It is also crucial to surround yourself with supportive individuals who believe in your potential. Seek out mentors, coaches, or friends who can provide guidance, encouragement, and constructive feedback. Their belief in you will act as a catalyst for your personal growth and help you overcome self-doubt.

In conclusion, nurturing a belief in personal growth and development is the key to achieving your best in life. By adopting a growth mindset, setting goals, and surrounding yourself with supportive individuals, you can overcome obstacles and build resilience. Embrace the idea that you have the power to grow and develop, and watch as your life transforms in remarkable ways.

Chapter 4: Strategies for Overcoming Obstacles

Building a Supportive Network

In the journey of achieving your best, it is essential to recognize the power of a supportive network. Surrounding yourself with individuals who uplift and inspire you can significantly impact your ability to overcome obstacles and build resilience in everyday life. This subchapter delves into the importance of building a supportive network and provides practical tips for cultivating meaningful connections.

Human beings are inherently social creatures, and having a strong support system is crucial for personal growth and success. A supportive network consists of people who genuinely care about your well-being, believe in your abilities, and are there to lend a helping hand when you need it most. Whether it's family, friends, mentors, or colleagues, these individuals can serve as pillars of strength and encouragement during challenging times.

One of the first steps in building a supportive network is identifying the people who align with your values and goals. Seek out individuals who inspire you to be your best self and who are willing to provide guidance and support along your journey. Additionally, it is essential to reciprocate this support by being equally present and uplifting in their lives. Building a network is a two-way street, and cultivating genuine relationships requires effort and commitment from both parties.

Another important aspect of building a supportive network is diversifying your connections. Surrounding yourself with people from different backgrounds, experiences, and areas of expertise can broaden your perspective and provide you with a wealth of knowledge and resources. Don't limit yourself to individuals who are similar to you. Embrace diversity and learn from others who may have different strengths and insights.

Furthermore, it is crucial to remember that building a supportive network is not just about receiving support but also offering it. Be willing to listen, empathize, and provide assistance when needed. By being a reliable and supportive friend, you create a reciprocal environment where everyone can thrive and grow together.

In conclusion, building a supportive network is an integral part of achieving your best and overcoming obstacles in everyday life. Surrounding yourself with individuals who uplift and inspire you, diversifying your connections, and reciprocating support are key components of cultivating a strong support system. Remember, resilience is not built in isolation but through the power of meaningful connections. Invest time and effort into building and nurturing your supportive network, and you will find yourself better equipped to bounce back from adversity and achieve your goals.

The importance of a strong support system

In our journey towards achieving our best, it's easy to underestimate the power of a strong support system. We often believe that success is solely dependent on our individual efforts and talents. However, the truth is that having a solid network of supportive individuals can greatly enhance our ability to overcome obstacles and build resilience in everyday life.

A strong support system provides us with the emotional and practical resources we need to face challenges head-on. When we encounter setbacks or failures, it is our network of friends, family, mentors, and colleagues who can offer guidance, encouragement, and a fresh perspective. They remind us of our strengths, help us see the bigger picture, and provide valuable insights that we may have overlooked. Their unwavering belief in our abilities fuels our motivation and helps us bounce back stronger than ever.

Moreover, a support system helps us maintain a positive mindset. Surrounding ourselves with individuals who share our values and aspirations creates an environment that fosters growth and positivity. They inspire us, challenge us, and push us to reach new heights. When we stumble or feel discouraged, they are there to remind us of our potential and keep us focused on our goals. Their unwavering support acts as a safety net, allowing us to take risks and step outside our comfort zones with confidence.

Furthermore, a strong support system provides us with valuable resources and opportunities. Through their connections and experiences, our network can offer insights, advice, and even mentorship that can accelerate our progress. They may introduce us to new career opportunities, provide recommendations, or share valuable information that can give us a competitive edge. By leveraging the expertise and connections of our support system, we can achieve our best more efficiently and effectively.

In conclusion, a strong support system is paramount in achieving our best. It provides us with emotional support, helps us maintain a positive mindset, and offers valuable resources and opportunities. By surrounding ourselves with individuals who believe in us and our potential, we can overcome obstacles, bounce back from setbacks, and build resilience in our everyday lives. So, let's nurture and invest in our support system, for it is the backbone that propels us towards our highest achievements.

Cultivating healthy relationships and seeking help when needed

In the pursuit of achieving our best, it is essential to understand the power of cultivating healthy relationships and seeking help when needed. Life is not meant to be lived in isolation, and having a strong support system is vital for personal growth and resilience.

Building and maintaining healthy relationships is a fundamental aspect of living a fulfilling life. Whether it is with family, friends, colleagues, or romantic partners, these connections provide us with emotional support, encouragement, and a sense of belonging. By investing time and effort into nurturing these relationships, we create a foundation of trust, love, and understanding that can withstand the challenges life throws our way.

However, it is equally important to recognize the need for help and support when faced with difficulties. No one is immune to setbacks or obstacles, and seeking assistance is not a sign of weakness but rather a sign of strength. Whether it is professional help, such as therapy or counseling, or seeking advice from a trusted mentor or friend, reaching out for support can provide us with new perspectives, guidance, and tools to overcome the challenges we face.

In our journey of achieving our best, it is crucial to remember that resilience is not a solitary endeavor. It is through the collective efforts of our support system that we can bounce back from setbacks, learn from our failures, and continue moving forward. By allowing ourselves to be vulnerable and seek help when needed, we open ourselves up to new opportunities, personal growth, and the ability to overcome any obstacle that comes our way.

Being proactive in cultivating healthy relationships and seeking help when needed requires self-awareness, empathy, and vulnerability. It means actively listening to others, offering support when necessary, and recognizing our own limitations. It also means being open to feedback, self-reflection, and personal growth.

As we navigate through life, let us remember that achieving our best is not solely about personal accomplishments, but also about the quality of our relationships and our willingness to seek help when needed. By cultivating healthy relationships and not being afraid to ask for assistance, we can build resilience, overcome obstacles, and ultimately live a more fulfilling and resilient life.

Practicing Self-Care

In our fast-paced and demanding world, it's easy to get caught up in the hustle and bustle of everyday life. We often prioritize our work, responsibilities, and obligations over our own well-being. However, in order to achieve our best and overcome obstacles, it is crucial to make self-care a priority.

Self-care is not a luxury; it is a necessity for our physical, mental, and emotional well-being. It involves taking deliberate actions to nurture and care for ourselves. By practicing self-care, we can recharge, rejuvenate, and build resilience to face whatever challenges come our way.

One of the fundamental aspects of self-care is prioritizing our physical health. This includes getting regular exercise, eating nutritious meals, and getting enough sleep. Physical activity not only boosts our energy levels but also improves our mood and enhances our overall well-being. Additionally, following a balanced diet and ensuring adequate rest are essential for maintaining a healthy body and mind.

Another crucial aspect of self-care is nurturing our mental and emotional health. It's important to carve out time for activities that bring us joy and relaxation. Whether it's reading a book, listening to music, practicing mindfulness, or engaging in a hobby, allocating time for activities that bring us happiness is essential for our mental well-being. Additionally, seeking support from loved ones or professional therapists can provide a safe space to express our emotions and work through any challenges we may be facing.

Self-care also involves setting boundaries and learning to say no. It is crucial to recognize our limits and not overextend ourselves. By establishing healthy boundaries, we can prevent burnout and ensure that we have enough time and energy to take care of ourselves.

Lastly, self-care includes practicing self-compassion and self-acceptance. It's important to be kind to ourselves and acknowledge that we are doing the best we can. Instead of being overly critical or judgmental, we should treat ourselves with the same compassion and understanding that we offer to others.

In conclusion, practicing self-care is a vital component of achieving our best and building resilience. By prioritizing our physical, mental, and emotional well-being, we can bounce back from obstacles and thrive in our everyday lives. Remember, self-care is not selfish; it is a necessary investment in ourselves that enables us to be the best version of ourselves for both our own benefit and for others around us.

Prioritizing physical and mental well-being

In our fast-paced and demanding world, it is easy to get caught up in the pursuit of success and overlook our own well-being. We often find ourselves sacrificing sleep, exercise, and self-care to meet deadlines and fulfill responsibilities. However, maintaining good physical and mental health is crucial for achieving our best in all aspects of life.

Physical well-being forms the foundation for a healthy and resilient lifestyle. It encompasses regular exercise, a balanced diet, and sufficient rest. Engaging in physical activities not only improves our physical health but also boosts our mental well-being. Exercise releases endorphins, the feel-good hormones, which not only reduce stress but also enhance our mood and overall happiness. Prioritizing physical fitness has been proven to increase productivity, focus, and creativity, enabling us to perform at our peak.

Mental well-being is equally important as physical health. It involves taking care of our emotional and psychological state. In today's high-pressure environments, stress, anxiety, and burnout are common challenges. Prioritizing mental well-being means finding ways to manage stress, practicing self-care, and seeking support when needed. This may involve engaging in relaxation techniques such as meditation, mindfulness, or hobbies that bring joy and relaxation. It also means setting boundaries, saying no when necessary, and creating space for self-reflection and personal growth.

When we prioritize our physical and mental well-being, we create a solid foundation for achieving our best. By taking care of our bodies and minds, we build resilience to face life's challenges head-on. We become more adaptable, resourceful, and better equipped to bounce back from setbacks. Moreover, by prioritizing self-care, we demonstrate self-love and self-respect, setting an example for others to do the same.

Incorporating physical and mental well-being into our daily lives doesn't have to be complicated. Small, consistent steps can make a significant difference. Start by incorporating short bursts of physical activity throughout the day, such as taking the stairs instead of the elevator or going for a walk during lunch breaks. Make conscious choices about the food you consume, opting for whole, nourishing meals. Prioritize sleep and ensure you get enough rest to recharge and rejuvenate.

Remember, achieving your best requires a holistic approach to well-being. By prioritizing physical and mental health, you are investing in yourself and creating a strong foundation for resilience and success. Start today, and watch how your overall well-being and ability to bounce back from obstacles soar to new heights.

Prioritizing Physical and Mental Well-being: Achieving Your Best

In our fast-paced and demanding world, it is easy to neglect our physical and mental well-being. We often find ourselves caught up in the pursuit of success, constantly striving to achieve our best. However, true success and resilience can only be built upon a foundation of good health and well-being. In this subchapter, we will explore the importance of prioritizing physical and mental well-being and provide practical strategies to help you achieve your best.

Physical well-being is the cornerstone of a healthy and resilient life. Taking care of your body is not just about looking good; it is about feeling good and performing at your peak. Regular exercise, proper nutrition, and sufficient rest are essential components of physical well-being. Engaging in physical activities that you enjoy, such as jogging, swimming, or practicing yoga, can help reduce stress, improve your mood, and boost your energy levels. Additionally, incorporating a balanced diet and ensuring you get enough sleep will enhance your overall well-being and provide the necessary fuel for your body to function optimally.

Equally important is the aspect of mental well-being. Our minds are powerful tools that can either propel us forward or hold us back. Prioritizing mental well-being involves nurturing a positive mindset, managing stress effectively, and seeking support when needed. Cultivating a positive mindset involves practicing gratitude, reframing negative thoughts, and embracing self-compassion. By doing so, you can build resilience and bounce back from life's challenges more easily.

Managing stress is crucial in achieving your best. Chronic stress can have detrimental effects on both your physical and mental health. It is essential to develop healthy coping mechanisms, such as mindfulness meditation, deep breathing exercises, or engaging in hobbies that bring you joy. Taking breaks and setting boundaries are also vital in preventing burnout and maintaining a healthy work-life balance.

Furthermore, seeking support when needed is a sign of strength, not weakness. Surrounding yourself with a supportive network of friends, family, or professionals can provide you with valuable guidance, encouragement, and perspective. Additionally, engaging in activities that promote relaxation and self-care, such as reading, listening to music, or spending time in nature, can help rejuvenate your mind and promote mental well-being.

Ultimately, achieving your best involves recognizing the importance of prioritizing physical and mental well-being. By taking care of your body and mind, you lay the foundation for resilience, success, and a fulfilling life. Remember, it is not selfish to prioritize your well-being; it is necessary for your overall growth and happiness.

Strategies for self-care and stress management

In our fast-paced and demanding world, taking care of ourselves and managing stress has become more important than ever. It is essential to prioritize self-care and develop effective strategies to maintain our well-being and achieve our best in all aspects of life. This subchapter will explore various strategies for self-care and stress management that can help us bounce back from obstacles and build resilience in everyday life.

1. Prioritize self-care: Start by recognizing that self-care is not selfish; it is necessary for our overall well-being. Make time for activities that bring you joy and relaxation, such as exercise, hobbies, spending time with loved ones, or engaging in self-reflection.

2. Practice mindfulness: Incorporate mindfulness into your daily routine. Mindfulness helps us stay present, reduce stress, and improve focus. Techniques like deep breathing, meditation, or journaling can be effective tools for managing stress and achieving a sense of balance.

3. Set boundaries: Learn to say no when necessary and establish healthy boundaries in your personal and professional life. Overcommitting can lead to burnout and increased stress levels. Prioritize tasks and delegate when possible to avoid feeling overwhelmed.

4. Engage in self-reflection: Take time to reflect on your emotions, thoughts, and reactions to various situations. Understanding our triggers and patterns can enable us to respond more effectively to stressors and build resilience.

5. Cultivate a support network: Surround yourself with positive and supportive individuals who uplift and encourage you. Share your challenges and seek advice from trusted friends, family members, or mentors. Remember, seeking support is a sign of strength, not weakness.

6. Practice self-compassion: Treat yourself with kindness and compassion during difficult times. Acknowledge that setbacks and mistakes are a part of life, and be gentle with yourself. Celebrate your achievements and practice positive self-talk.

7. Take care of your physical health: Ensure you are getting enough sleep, eating a balanced diet, and engaging in regular exercise. Taking care of your physical health not only improves your energy levels but also enhances your ability to manage stress.

By implementing these strategies for self-care and stress management, you can achieve your best in all areas of life. Remember, building resilience requires consistent effort and practice. Embrace these techniques as lifelong tools to support your well-being and bounce back from any obstacles that come your way. Start prioritizing yourself today, and watch as your resilience and ability to overcome challenges soar to new heights.

In today's fast-paced world, it is essential to prioritize self-care and stress management in order to achieve your best and live a fulfilling life. In this subchapter, we will explore effective strategies that can help you bounce back from obstacles and build resilience in your everyday life.

1. Prioritize physical well-being: Taking care of your body is crucial for overall well-being. Engage in regular exercise, eat a balanced diet, and get enough sleep. This not only boosts your physical health but also enhances your mental and emotional resilience.

2. Practice mindfulness and relaxation techniques: Incorporating mindfulness into your daily routine can significantly reduce stress levels. Set aside a few minutes each day for deep breathing exercises, meditation, or yoga. These practices help you stay focused, calm, and present, enabling you to handle challenges more effectively.

3. Set boundaries and learn to say no: It's important to recognize your limits and set boundaries to protect your mental and emotional health. Learn to say no to additional commitments that overwhelm you or distract you from your goals. Prioritize your own well-being and allocate time for activities that rejuvenate and bring you joy.

4. Cultivate a support network: Surrounding yourself with positive and supportive individuals can help you navigate challenges more effectively. Foster relationships with people who uplift and inspire you. Seek support from friends, family, or even professional counselors when needed. Sharing your experiences and emotions with others can offer fresh perspectives and valuable guidance.

5. Engage in self-reflection and self-care activities: Regular self-reflection allows you to assess your emotions, thoughts, and behaviors. This awareness enables you to identify triggers and develop coping mechanisms. Engage in activities that bring you joy and relaxation, such as hobbies, reading, or spending time in nature. Taking time for yourself replenishes your energy and enhances your overall resilience.

6. Practice time management and goal setting: Effective time management allows you to prioritize tasks and reduce stress. Set realistic goals and break them down into smaller, manageable steps. This approach not only helps you stay organized but also boosts your confidence and motivation as you achieve each milestone.

Remember, self-care and stress management are ongoing processes that require consistent effort and practice. By implementing these strategies into your daily routine, you can enhance your resilience, overcome obstacles, and achieve your best in all areas of life. Take the first step towards a more fulfilling and resilient future today!

Chapter 5: Resilience in Action

Learning from Resilient Individuals

In our journey through life, we often encounter obstacles and face challenges that test our resilience. But what if we could learn from those who have mastered the art of bouncing back? In this subchapter, we will explore the valuable lessons we can glean from resilient individuals and how we can apply them to achieve our best.

Resilient individuals possess a unique set of qualities that enable them to overcome adversity and thrive in the face of obstacles. One key attribute they possess is a positive mindset. They understand that setbacks are a part of life and view them as opportunities for growth and learning. By adopting this mindset, we can reframe our challenges and see them as stepping stones towards achieving our best.

Another trait resilient individuals possess is the ability to adapt to change. Life is dynamic, and being able to navigate through unexpected twists and turns is crucial. Resilient individuals embrace change and view it as a chance for personal and professional development. By learning to adapt, we can become more flexible and open to new opportunities, ultimately propelling us towards achieving our best.

Furthermore, resilient individuals possess strong support networks. They understand the importance of surrounding themselves with positive and supportive individuals who uplift and motivate them during difficult times. By cultivating our own support networks, we can lean on them for guidance, encouragement, and inspiration when we face challenges.

Resilient individuals also take care of their physical and mental well-being. They prioritize self-care and understand that their ability to overcome obstacles is directly linked to their overall health. By incorporating practices such as exercise, mindfulness, and self-reflection into our daily lives, we can build the resilience needed to achieve our best.

Learning from resilient individuals is not just about emulating their qualities; it is also about studying their journeys. By examining their stories of triumph and resilience, we can gain insights into the strategies and mindset that helped them overcome adversity. Through their experiences, we can learn valuable lessons and apply them to our own lives.

In conclusion, learning from resilient individuals can provide us with invaluable tools and insights to achieve our best. By adopting a positive mindset, embracing change, nurturing support networks, and prioritizing our well-being, we can build the resilience necessary to overcome obstacles and thrive in every aspect of our lives. So, let us embark on this journey of learning, drawing inspiration from those who have already mastered the art of bouncing back, and become the best version of ourselves.

Resilience is a quality that we all aspire to possess. When faced with challenges and obstacles, resilient individuals display an exceptional ability to bounce back and overcome adversity. In the subchapter "Learning from Resilient Individuals" from the book "Bouncing Back:

Overcoming Obstacles and Building Resilience in Everyday Life," we delve into the inspiring stories of those who have mastered the art of resilience. By examining their experiences and strategies, we can learn valuable lessons to help us achieve our best in life.

Resilient individuals come from all walks of life, and their stories demonstrate that anyone can cultivate resilience. They have faced setbacks, failures, and hardships, yet they managed to emerge stronger and more determined. Their journeys remind us that resilience is not an innate trait but rather a skill that can be cultivated and honed.

One crucial lesson we can learn from resilient individuals is the power of mindset. They possess an unwavering belief in their abilities and refuse to be defined by their setbacks. Instead of dwelling on their failures, they focus on the lessons learned and seek opportunities for growth. They understand that setbacks are not permanent roadblocks but merely temporary hurdles on the path to success.

Another key aspect of resilience is the ability to adapt and remain flexible in the face of adversity. Resilient individuals understand that life is unpredictable and constantly changing. They embrace change and view it as an opportunity for growth and self-improvement. By being open to new possibilities and adjusting their strategies, they can navigate through challenging situations more effectively.

Furthermore, resilient individuals have a strong support system. They surround themselves with positive and like-minded individuals who provide encouragement, guidance, and support during difficult times. They understand the importance of seeking help when needed and are not afraid to lean on others for support. Building a network of supportive individuals can significantly contribute to one's ability to bounce back from setbacks.

Finally, resilient individuals practice self-care and prioritize their well-being. They understand that to reach their full potential, they must take care of their physical, emotional, and mental health. By engaging in activities that promote relaxation, self-reflection, and self-care, they recharge their energy and maintain a positive outlook, even in the face of adversity.

In conclusion, learning from resilient individuals is a powerful way to enhance our own resilience and achieve our best in life. By adopting their mindset, embracing change, seeking support, and prioritizing self-care, we can overcome obstacles and bounce back stronger than ever. Resilience is not an unattainable trait reserved for a select few, but rather a skill that can be developed by anyone willing to learn and grow. Let the stories of resilient individuals inspire and guide you on your own journey towards achieving your best.

Inspiring stories of individuals who have overcome significant obstacles

Title: Inspiring Stories of Individuals Who Have Overcome Significant Obstacles

Introduction:

In the face of adversity, some individuals possess an unwavering spirit that enables them to rise above the challenges and emerge stronger than ever before. These inspiring stories of remarkable individuals who have overcome significant obstacles serve as a testament to the power of resilience and determination. In this subchapter, we delve into the lives of these extraordinary individuals, offering valuable insights and motivation to help you achieve your best.

1. Triumphing against Physical Limitations: Meet Sarah, a young woman who lost her legs in a tragic accident but refused to let her disability define her. Through sheer determination, she not only learned to walk again with prosthetic legs but also became an accomplished athlete, participating in marathons and inspiring others with her indomitable spirit. Sarah's story reminds us that our physical limitations do not have to limit our dreams.

2. Overcoming Personal Tragedy: John's life was shattered when he lost his wife and children in a devastating house fire. Grief-stricken and broken, he could have succumbed to despair. However, he chose to honor their memory by starting a charity that provides support and resources to families affected by similar tragedies. John's story teaches us that even in the

darkest moments, we can find the strength to turn our pain into purpose.

3.   Rising   Above   Financial   Adversity:
Maria grew up in poverty, facing countless obstacles on her journey to success. With determination and a relentless work ethic, she managed to overcome her challenging circumstances and became a successful entrepreneur. By sharing her experiences and offering practical tips, Maria's story encourages individuals to believe in their own potential and seize opportunities to achieve financial stability.

4.   Conquering   Mental   Health   Challenges:
Ryan battled with depression and anxiety for years, struggling to find a way forward. Through therapy, self-reflection, and an unwavering support system, he learned to take control of his mental health. Today, Ryan's story serves as a beacon of hope for countless others who face similar challenges, reminding us that seeking help is a sign of strength and that recovery is possible.

Conclusion:
These incredible stories of resilience and determination remind us that we all have the power to overcome obstacles, no matter how significant they may seem. By learning from the experiences of these inspiring individuals, we can find the motivation and strength to achieve our best. Remember, every setback is an opportunity for growth, and every obstacle can be transformed into a stepping stone towards success. Let these stories ignite your spirit and inspire you to overcome any hurdle that comes your way.

Subchapter: Inspiring Stories of Individuals Who Have Overcome Significant Obstacles

Introduction:
In life, we all face obstacles and challenges that can threaten to derail our dreams and aspirations. However, it is in these moments of adversity that our true character and strength are revealed. In this subchapter, we will explore the inspiring stories of individuals who have faced significant obstacles and triumphed over them, demonstrating the power of resilience and determination.

1.   Emma's   Journey   to   Empowerment:
Emma, a young woman born with a physical disability, faced numerous obstacles throughout her life. Despite societal limitations and discouragement, she refused to let her circumstances define her. Emma pursued her passion for art and became an influential painter, using her creativity as a means of self-expression. Through her art, she inspired countless others facing adversity to embrace their unique abilities and overcome challenges.

2.   John's   Road   to   Recovery:
John, a successful entrepreneur, experienced a devastating setback when his business collapsed during an economic crisis. Overwhelmed by financial losses and personal hardships, he found himself at rock bottom. Instead of giving up, John made a conscious choice to rebuild his life. He sought support from mentors, engaged in self-reflection, and developed a new business strategy. Today, he not only recovered but became even more successful, inspiring others to persevere in the face of failure.

3.   Sarah's   Triumph   Over   Trauma:

Sarah survived a traumatic event that left her emotionally scarred and afraid to trust again. Determined to reclaim her life, she embarked on a journey of healing and self-discovery. Through therapy, support groups, and her unwavering determination, Sarah not only overcame her trauma but also became an advocate for survivors. Her story serves as a beacon of hope for those struggling with their own traumatic experiences, proving that healing and resilience are possible.

Conclusion:

These stories of individuals overcoming significant obstacles serve as powerful reminders that our circumstances do not define us. They demonstrate that with resilience, determination, and the support of others, we can rise above any challenge. Whether it is physical limitations, business failures, or emotional trauma, these stories inspire us to believe in our own capacity to achieve greatness. By learning from these individuals' experiences, we can find the strength to face our own obstacles and strive for our best, no matter what life throws our way.

Lessons learned and key takeaways

In the journey of life, we often encounter obstacles that test our strength and resilience. It is during these challenging times that we learn valuable lessons and gain important insights that help us bounce back stronger than ever before. In the book "Bouncing Back: Overcoming Obstacles and Building Resilience in Everyday Life," we explore the various lessons learned and key takeaways that can help us achieve our best and overcome any hurdle that comes our way.

One of the fundamental lessons we learn is the power of a positive mindset. Maintaining a positive outlook in the face of adversity can make all the difference. By shifting our perspective and focusing on the opportunities hidden within challenges, we can find the motivation and strength to push forward. The book emphasizes the importance of cultivating resilience, which enables us to adapt, grow, and thrive in the face of adversity.

Another key takeaway from the book is the significance of self-care. Taking care of ourselves physically, mentally, and emotionally is vital in achieving our best. The book provides practical strategies for self-care, including setting boundaries, practicing mindfulness, and nurturing positive relationships. By prioritizing self-care, we can recharge our energy and build the resilience needed to overcome obstacles.

Furthermore, "Bouncing Back" highlights the importance of perseverance and never giving up. The book shares inspiring stories of individuals who faced numerous setbacks but persisted until they achieved their goals. It emphasizes that setbacks are not permanent and that success often comes after multiple failures. Through determination and perseverance, we can overcome obstacles and achieve our best.

The book also underscores the significance of learning from failures and setbacks. Each setback provides an opportunity for growth and learning. By analyzing our failures and understanding the lessons they teach us, we can refine our strategies and move closer to our goals. "Bouncing Back" provides practical guidance on how to turn failures into stepping stones towards success.

In conclusion, "Bouncing Back: Overcoming Obstacles and Building Resilience in Everyday Life" offers valuable lessons and key takeaways for achieving our best. By cultivating a positive mindset, prioritizing self-care, persevering through challenges, and learning from failures, we can overcome any obstacle and build the resilience necessary for success. This book serves as a guide for individuals from all walks of life, reminding us that resilience is not just about bouncing back, but also about bouncing forward and achieving our fullest potential.

In the journey of life, we often encounter obstacles that challenge our ability to achieve our best. However, it is during these moments of adversity that we have the opportunity to bounce back and build resilience. The book, "Bouncing Back: Overcoming Obstacles and Building Resilience in Everyday Life," offers valuable lessons and key takeaways for everyone striving to live their best lives.

One of the most important lessons learned from this book is the power of reframing challenges as opportunities for growth. Often, we view obstacles as setbacks or barriers to our success. However, the author encourages us to shift our mindset and see these challenges as stepping stones to resilience. By reframing our perspective, we can transform setbacks into opportunities for personal development and growth.

Another key takeaway from the book is the importance of self-belief and optimism. It highlights the significance of having faith in our abilities and maintaining a positive outlook, even in the face of adversity. The author emphasizes that resilience is not about avoiding failure or hardship but about having the resilience to bounce back stronger and wiser.

The book also delves into the concept of building a support system. It highlights the significance of surrounding ourselves with positive and like-minded individuals who can provide encouragement and support during difficult times. The power of community and connection is emphasized as a vital tool in overcoming obstacles and achieving our best.

Furthermore, "Bouncing Back" emphasizes the importance of self-care and self-compassion. It reminds readers that taking care of our physical and mental well-being is crucial for building resilience. By prioritizing self-care, we can recharge and replenish our energy, enabling us to tackle challenges with greater strength and resilience.

Lastly, the book emphasizes the role of perseverance and determination in bouncing back from obstacles. It teaches us that setbacks are temporary and that with perseverance, we can overcome any hurdle. The author shares inspiring stories of individuals who have faced tremendous obstacles but managed to triumph through sheer determination and resilience.

In conclusion, "Bouncing Back: Overcoming Obstacles and Building Resilience in Everyday Life" offers valuable lessons and key takeaways for everyone striving to achieve their best. By reframing challenges, maintaining self-belief, building a support system, practicing self-care, and embracing perseverance, we can cultivate resilience and overcome any obstacle that comes our way. This book serves as a guide to help individuals navigate the ups and downs of life and emerge stronger, more resilient, and capable of achieving their best.

Applying Resilience in Everyday Life

Resilience is a powerful trait that can help us overcome obstacles and thrive in our everyday lives. It is not just limited to the extraordinary individuals who have faced adversity and emerged stronger; it is a skill that can be developed and applied by anyone. In this subchapter, we will explore how to apply resilience in our everyday lives for achieving our best.

One of the key aspects of applying resilience is understanding that challenges and setbacks are a natural part of life. Instead of viewing them as roadblocks, we can choose to see them as opportunities for growth and learning. By adopting a positive mindset and embracing the belief that we have the strength to overcome any obstacle, we can navigate through life's challenges with confidence.

Another crucial factor in applying resilience is practicing self-care. Taking care of ourselves physically, mentally, and emotionally is essential for building resilience. This includes maintaining a healthy lifestyle, engaging in activities that bring us joy and fulfillment, and seeking support from our loved ones when needed. By prioritizing self-care, we are better equipped to handle the ups and downs of life.

Additionally, cultivating a strong support system is vital for applying resilience. Surrounding ourselves with positive and supportive individuals who believe in our abilities can greatly impact our resilience levels. Their encouragement and guidance can help us maintain a sense of perspective, provide valuable insights, and boost our confidence during challenging times.

Resilience also involves setting realistic goals and managing expectations. By breaking down our objectives into smaller, achievable steps, we can work towards our goals while acknowledging our progress along the way. This approach allows us to maintain motivation and momentum, even when faced with setbacks.

Lastly, embracing failure as a stepping stone towards success is a crucial aspect of applying resilience. Instead of viewing failure as a reflection of our worth or abilities, we can choose to see it as an opportunity to learn, grow, and improve. By reframing failure as a valuable lesson rather than a personal defeat, we can bounce back stronger and wiser.

In conclusion, resilience is a skill that can be applied in our everyday lives to help us achieve our best. By adopting a positive mindset, practicing self-care, cultivating a support system, setting realistic goals, and embracing failure, we can navigate through life's challenges with resilience and emerge stronger than ever before. So, let's embrace resilience as a guiding principle and unlock our true potential.

Resilience is the remarkable ability to bounce back from adversity, overcome obstacles, and thrive in the face of challenges. It is a crucial skill that can empower individuals to achieve their best in every aspect of life. In this subchapter, we will explore how resilience can be applied in our everyday lives to enhance our well-being, personal growth, and overall success.

One of the key ways to apply resilience in everyday life is by embracing a positive mindset. By cultivating optimism and focusing on solutions rather than dwelling on problems, we can navigate through difficult situations with greater ease. This mindset shift allows us to see setbacks as opportunities for growth and learning, enabling us to develop new strategies and improve our chances of success.

Additionally, resilience involves building strong support networks. Surrounding ourselves with positive, like-minded individuals who uplift and encourage us can make a significant difference in our ability to overcome challenges. By seeking support from friends, family, mentors, or even professional networks, we can gain valuable perspectives, advice, and emotional support that can help us navigate through tough times.

Resilience is also closely linked to self-care and well-being. Taking care of our physical, mental, and emotional health is crucial in maintaining resilience. Engaging in activities that bring us joy, practicing mindfulness or meditation, exercising regularly, and ensuring adequate rest are all essential components of self-care. By prioritizing our well-being, we can build the resilience needed to tackle life's obstacles head-on.

Moreover, setting realistic goals and maintaining a sense of purpose can contribute to our resilience. By breaking down larger goals into smaller, achievable steps, we can maintain motivation and momentum even when faced with setbacks. Having a clear sense of purpose also provides a guiding light during challenging times, reminding us of our values and what truly matters to us.

In conclusion, applying resilience in our everyday lives is crucial for achieving our best. By cultivating a positive mindset, building strong support networks, prioritizing self-care, and setting realistic goals, we can navigate through obstacles with resilience and emerge stronger than ever before. Remember, resilience is not about avoiding challenges but rather about embracing them and using them as stepping stones to personal growth and success. So, embrace your inner strength, face adversity head-on, and watch yourself bounce back and achieve your best in every aspect of life.

Practical tips for applying resilience in various areas of life (work, relationships, personal growth)

Resilience is a powerful trait that can help us overcome obstacles and navigate through the ups and downs of life. In today's fast-paced and ever-changing world, building resilience has become essential for achieving personal growth, maintaining healthy relationships, and excelling in our professional lives. In this subchapter, we will explore practical tips for applying resilience in various areas of life, including work, relationships, and personal growth.

When it comes to work, resilience is crucial for achieving your best. Start by setting realistic goals and breaking them down into smaller, manageable tasks. This will help you stay focused and motivated, even when faced with setbacks. Embrace challenges as opportunities for growth and learning, and maintain a positive mindset to overcome obstacles along the way. Practice effective time management, prioritize tasks, and create a healthy work-life balance to avoid burnout. Remember to celebrate your achievements, no matter how small, as this will boost your confidence and resilience.

In relationships, resilience plays a vital role in maintaining harmony and connection. Cultivate open and honest communication with your loved ones, expressing your needs and concerns while actively listening to theirs. When conflicts arise, approach them with empathy and understanding, seeking compromise and finding common ground. Building resilience in relationships means being adaptable and willing to change, as well as practicing forgiveness and letting go of grudges. Remember that conflict is a natural part of any relationship, and it can be an opportunity for growth and deeper connection.

Personal growth requires resilience to overcome challenges and achieve your full potential. Embrace a growth mindset, believing in your ability to learn and improve. Set realistic and achievable goals that align with your values and passions, and break them down into actionable steps. Embrace failure as a steppingstone to success, learning from your mistakes and persevering even when things get tough. Surround yourself with a supportive network of friends, mentors, or like-minded individuals who can provide guidance and encouragement along your personal growth journey.

In conclusion, resilience is a key factor in achieving your best in various areas of life. By applying practical tips in work, relationships, and personal growth, you can bounce back from setbacks and thrive in the face of adversity. Remember to stay focused, maintain a positive mindset, and cultivate healthy habits that support your resilience. With these tools, you can overcome obstacles and build a life filled with growth, success, and meaningful connections.

Resilience is the ability to bounce back from challenges, setbacks, and adversity. It is a critical skill that can help us overcome obstacles, achieve our goals, and lead a more fulfilling life. In this subchapter, we will explore practical tips for applying resilience in various areas of life, including work, relationships, and personal growth. These tips can be implemented by anyone who aspires to achieve their best and build a resilient mindset.

1.   Work:
- Embrace a growth mindset: View challenges as opportunities for growth and learning. Instead of getting discouraged by setbacks, approach them as stepping stones towards success.

- Set realistic goals: Break down your goals into smaller, manageable tasks. This will not only make them less overwhelming but also allow you to celebrate small wins along the way.
- Seek support: Cultivate a strong support system at work. Surround yourself with positive and like-minded individuals who can provide guidance, encouragement, and help you navigate through difficult times.

2. Relationships:
- Practice empathy and active listening: Show genuine interest in others' perspectives and feelings. Being empathetic and actively listening can foster stronger connections and understanding in your relationships.
- Communicate effectively: Clearly express your thoughts and emotions while being open to feedback. Effective communication can prevent misunderstandings and strengthen interpersonal bonds.
- Set healthy boundaries: Understand your limits and communicate them to others. Setting boundaries can help maintain a healthy balance in your relationships and prevent burnout.

3. Personal Growth:
- Prioritize self-care: Take care of your physical, mental, and emotional well-being. Engage in activities that bring you joy, practice self-compassion, and strive for a healthy work-life balance.
- Cultivate a positive mindset: Focus on the positive aspects of your life and practice gratitude. Optimism and gratitude can help you maintain a resilient attitude during challenging times.
- Embrace failure as a learning opportunity: Instead of fearing failure, see it as a chance to learn and grow. Embracing failure can lead to personal development and new opportunities.

Remember, building resilience takes time and effort. By implementing these practical tips in various areas of your life, you can develop a resilient mindset that will allow you to overcome obstacles, achieve your best, and lead a more fulfilling life.

Setting goals and taking action towards resilience

In today's fast-paced and challenging world, it is essential to develop the skill of resilience in order to overcome obstacles and achieve our best. Resilience is the ability to bounce back from setbacks, to adapt to change, and to persevere in the face of adversity. It is a quality that can be cultivated and honed through setting goals and taking deliberate action.

Setting goals is the first step towards building resilience. When we have a clear vision of what we want to achieve, it becomes easier to navigate through the ups and downs of life. Goals provide us with a sense of purpose and direction, serving as a guiding light during difficult times. They give us something to strive for and help us stay focused and motivated.

To set effective goals, it is important to make them specific, measurable, achievable, relevant, and time-bound (SMART). By breaking down our larger goals into smaller, manageable steps, we can make progress and build momentum. Each small achievement brings us closer to our ultimate objective, boosting our confidence and resilience along the way.

Taking action is the next crucial step towards resilience. It is not enough to simply set goals; we must also be willing to take consistent and determined action towards them. This requires discipline, perseverance, and a willingness to step out of our comfort zones. Taking action may involve facing fears, making sacrifices, and embracing uncertainty. However, it is through these actions that we build resilience and develop the strength to overcome any obstacles that come our way.

In order to achieve our best, it is important to remember that resilience is not a destination but a lifelong journey. It requires continuous effort and an unwavering commitment to personal growth. Along the way, we may encounter setbacks, failures, and disappointments. However, by setting goals and taking action towards resilience, we can learn from these experiences, adapt, and come back stronger than ever.

In conclusion, setting goals and taking action towards resilience is crucial for achieving our best in life. By setting clear and specific goals, breaking them down into manageable steps, and consistently taking action, we can build the resilience necessary to overcome any obstacles and thrive in our everyday lives. Remember, resilience is not about avoiding challenges, but about embracing them and using them as stepping stones towards personal growth and success. So, set your goals, take action, and bounce back stronger than ever!

In our journey towards achieving our best, we often encounter obstacles and setbacks that can leave us feeling defeated and discouraged. However, it is during these challenging moments that our resilience is truly tested. Resilience is the ability to bounce back from adversity, to adapt and thrive in the face of difficulties. It is not something that we are born with, but rather a skill that can be developed and honed over time.

To build resilience, one of the key steps is setting goals and taking action. Goals provide us with a sense of purpose and direction, giving us something to strive towards. They act as a roadmap, guiding us through the ups and downs of life, and helping us stay focused on the bigger picture.

When setting goals, it is important to make them specific, measurable, achievable, relevant, and time-bound (SMART). This ensures that our goals are realistic and attainable, allowing us to experience a sense of progress and accomplishment along the way. For example, if your goal is to improve your physical fitness, a SMART goal could be to run a 5k race within the next three months.

Once we have set our goals, the next step is to take action. This involves breaking down our goals into smaller, manageable tasks and creating a plan of action. By taking small steps consistently, we can make progress towards our goals and build momentum. It is important to remember that progress is not always linear, and setbacks are a natural part of the process. However, by staying committed and determined, we can overcome these setbacks and continue moving forward.

Taking action also involves developing a positive mindset and cultivating resilience. It requires us to challenge our limiting beliefs and replace them with empowering thoughts. It involves practicing self-compassion and embracing self-care, as taking care of our physical and mental well-being is crucial in maintaining resilience.

In conclusion, setting goals and taking action towards resilience is a powerful tool in achieving our best. By setting SMART goals, breaking them down into actionable steps, and developing a positive mindset, we can overcome obstacles and build resilience in everyday life.

Remember, resilience is not about avoiding failure or adversity, but rather about how we respond and bounce back from it. So, let us embrace the journey, set our goals, and take action towards becoming the best version of ourselves.

Conclusion

Recap of key concepts and strategies discussed

In this subchapter, we will summarize the key concepts and strategies discussed throughout the book "Bouncing Back: Overcoming Obstacles and Building Resilience in Everyday Life." Whether you are an ambitious professional, a student, or simply someone seeking to achieve your best in life, this recap will provide you with a valuable overview.

Resilience, as we have learned, is the ability to adapt and recover from adversity, setbacks, and challenges. It is not about avoiding difficulties but rather about developing the strength to bounce back stronger than ever. To cultivate resilience, we must first embrace a growth mindset, believing that we can learn and grow from every experience, no matter how difficult.

The book emphasizes the importance of self-awareness as a foundation for resilience. Understanding our strengths, weaknesses, values, and passions enables us to set meaningful goals and make choices aligned with our authentic selves. Additionally, developing emotional intelligence allows us to manage our emotions, navigate relationships effectively, and respond to stress in a healthy manner.

Throughout the chapters, we have explored various strategies to build resilience. One such strategy is cultivating a positive mindset. By reframing negative thoughts, practicing gratitude, and focusing on strengths, we can maintain a positive outlook even in challenging times. Additionally, maintaining a healthy lifestyle that includes regular exercise, proper nutrition, and adequate sleep is crucial for our physical and mental well-being.

The book also delves into the significance of building a support network. Surrounding ourselves with positive, supportive individuals who share our goals and values can provide us with the encouragement and guidance we need to overcome obstacles. Furthermore, we have learned about the power of seeking help when necessary, as resilience does not mean facing challenges alone.

Lastly, the book emphasizes the importance of perseverance and adaptability. Resilient individuals understand that setbacks are inevitable, but they view them as opportunities for growth. They are willing to adapt their strategies, learn from failures, and continue moving forward despite obstacles.

In conclusion, "Bouncing Back: Overcoming Obstacles and Building Resilience in Everyday Life" has provided us with valuable insights into the key concepts and strategies for achieving our best. By adopting a growth mindset, cultivating self-awareness, practicing emotional intelligence, maintaining a positive mindset, building a support network, and embracing perseverance and adaptability, we can develop the resilience necessary to overcome any challenge and thrive in our personal and professional lives. Remember, resilience is a skill that can be learned and strengthened, and it is within everyone's reach.

In the previous chapters of "Bouncing Back: Overcoming Obstacles and Building Resilience in Everyday Life," we have explored various concepts and strategies that can help you overcome obstacles and build resilience in your everyday life. This subchapter serves as a recap of these key ideas and provides a comprehensive overview for those who may have missed any important points.

One of the fundamental concepts discussed in the book is the power of mindset. We emphasized the importance of adopting a growth mindset, which involves believing in your ability to learn and grow from challenges. By cultivating a growth mindset, you can develop resilience and bounce back stronger from setbacks.

Another key concept addressed is the significance of self-care. We explored various self-care strategies, including physical exercise, mindfulness practices, and maintaining a healthy work-life balance. Taking care of your physical and mental well-being is crucial for building resilience and achieving your best.

Moreover, we discussed the role of emotional intelligence in resilience. Understanding and managing your emotions, as well as empathizing with others, can greatly contribute to your ability to navigate through difficult situations. Developing emotional intelligence allows you to build stronger relationships and effectively cope with stress.

The book also delved into the importance of setting realistic goals and creating a plan of action. We explored strategies such as breaking down larger goals into smaller achievable tasks, setting SMART (Specific, Measurable, Achievable, Relevant, Time-bound) goals, and using visualization techniques to enhance motivation.

In addition, we examined the power of positive thinking and reframing negative experiences. By challenging negative thoughts and focusing on the positive aspects of a situation, you can cultivate a more optimistic outlook and enhance your resilience.

Throughout the book, we highlighted the significance of building a support network. Surrounding yourself with positive and supportive individuals can provide encouragement, motivation, and guidance during challenging times. We discussed the importance of seeking help when needed and not hesitating to lean on others for support.

Lastly, we explored strategies for maintaining resilience in the face of adversity. These included practicing self-compassion, embracing failure as a learning opportunity, embracing change, and developing problem-solving skills.

By incorporating these key concepts and strategies into your life, you can overcome obstacles and build resilience, ultimately achieving your best. Remember that resilience is a skill that can be developed and strengthened, and with practice, you can bounce back from any setback that comes your way.

Encouragement to continue building resilience in everyday life

Resilience is not just a trait possessed by a select few; it is a quality that can be cultivated by everyone. In the pursuit of achieving your best, it is crucial to understand the importance of resilience in overcoming obstacles and thriving in everyday life. This subchapter aims to provide encouragement and practical strategies to help you build and strengthen your resilience.

Life is seldom a smooth journey; it is filled with challenges, setbacks, and unexpected twists. However, it is through these trials that we have the opportunity to grow and develop our resilience. Resilience is not about avoiding adversity, but rather about bouncing back and adapting in the face of adversity. It is about harnessing our inner strength and finding the courage to persevere.

One of the most powerful ways to build resilience is by adopting a positive mindset. Challenges and setbacks can often leave us feeling defeated and demotivated. However, by reframing our perspective and focusing on the potential for growth and learning, we can turn these obstacles into opportunities. Embracing a growth mindset allows us to see setbacks as stepping stones towards success and encourages us to continue pushing forward.

Another crucial aspect of building resilience is developing a support system. Surrounding yourself with positive and uplifting individuals who believe in your abilities can make a world of difference. Having people who provide emotional support, offer guidance, and cheer you on during difficult times can help you stay motivated and maintain your resilience.

It is also essential to practice self-care and prioritize your well-being. Building resilience requires mental and physical strength, which can only be achieved when we take care of ourselves. Engaging in activities that bring you joy, practicing mindfulness and self-reflection, and maintaining a healthy lifestyle are all crucial components of building resilience.

Lastly, remember that resilience is not built overnight. It is a lifelong journey that requires consistent effort and practice. Embrace the setbacks and challenges as opportunities for growth, and never lose sight of your goals. Believe in yourself and your abilities, and know that you have the power to overcome any obstacle that comes your way.

In conclusion, building resilience is an essential aspect of achieving your best in life. By adopting a positive mindset, cultivating a support system, practicing self-care, and persevering through challenges, you can build and strengthen your resilience. Remember, resilience is not about avoiding adversity but about bouncing back and thriving despite it. Embrace the journey, stay determined, and never underestimate your own ability to overcome obstacles and achieve greatness.

Resilience is the key to overcoming obstacles and achieving your best in everyday life. It is the ability to bounce back from setbacks, adapt to challenges, and keep moving forward despite difficulties. In this subchapter, we will explore the importance of resilience and provide encouragement to continue building it in your life.

Life is filled with unexpected twists and turns. We all face setbacks, disappointments, and failures at some point. However, it is our response to these challenges that determines our success. Resilience allows us to face adversity head-on, learn from our experiences, and grow stronger in the process.

Building resilience requires a mindset shift. Instead of viewing setbacks as roadblocks, see them as opportunities for growth and self-improvement. Embrace the belief that every challenge is a chance to learn and become better. Remember that failure is not a reflection of your worth; it is simply a stepping stone on the path to success.

To build resilience, it is essential to cultivate a positive and optimistic outlook. Surround yourself with supportive people who uplift and inspire you. Seek out role models who have overcome similar obstacles and learn from their experiences. Remember, you are not alone in your journey, and there are others who have faced and conquered the same challenges you are facing.

In addition to mindset, building resilience also involves developing coping strategies. Find healthy ways to manage stress and emotions. Practice self-care, engage in activities that bring you joy, and prioritize your mental and physical well-being. Explore mindfulness and relaxation techniques to help you stay grounded during difficult times.

Celebrate your successes, no matter how small they may seem. Recognize the progress you have made and give yourself credit for your resilience. By acknowledging your achievements, you reinforce your belief in your ability to overcome obstacles and achieve your best.

Resilience is not a one-time achievement; it is a lifelong journey. It requires consistent effort and dedication. Remember that setbacks and challenges are a normal part of life, and building resilience is an ongoing process. Embrace each new obstacle as an opportunity to grow and develop your resilience further.

In conclusion, building resilience is crucial for achieving your best in everyday life. It enables you to bounce back from setbacks, adapt to challenges, and keep moving forward. By cultivating a positive mindset, seeking support, developing coping strategies, and celebrating your successes, you can continue building resilience and overcome any obstacle that comes your way. Remember, you have the power within you to overcome and thrive. Keep pushing forward, and you will discover the strength and resilience you never knew you had.

Milton Keynes UK
Ingram Content Group UK Ltd.
UKHW020925201123
432908UK00021B/3197